P   ⟨O⟩K OF

Elegance

The Modern Girl's Guide
to Living with Style

JODI KAHN

ILLUSTRATED BY KERREN BARBAS

PETER PAUPER PRESS, INC.
WHITE PLAINS, NEW YORK

*For David—the one thing in
my wardrobe I can't live without*

*And for Irene Winterberg and Ceil Samuels,
who wrote the book on elegance long ago*

Designed by Heather Zschock

Illustrations copyright © 2005 Kerren Barbas

Copyright © 2005
Peter Pauper Press, Inc.
202 Mamaroneck Avenue
White Plains, NY 10601
All rights reserved
ISBN 1-59359-999-4
Printed in Hong Kong
7 6 5 4 3 2 1

Visit us at www.peterpauper.com

THE LITTLE
PINK BOOK OF

Elegance

CONTENTS

INTRODUCTION

If you're like most women I know, you're probably trying to juggle a million things at once. Whether you're a mom, wife, working girl—or all three—you're probably doing the best you can just to make it through each day. And when you do manage to grab a moment for yourself, it's on the run—like gulping down a double latte in a paper cup on your way to soccer practice or your next meeting. So, you might wonder, who's got time for elegance? Is elegance even relevant in this day of e-mails and dress-down Fridays?

Don't worry. Modern elegance is not about squeezing one more thing into your already hectic schedule—it's about looking at things from a different perspective. It's about conducting your life in a way that lets you notice the beauty inside yourself, and in the world around you. Living elegantly is about adding a sparkle and a wink to your daily life, so that you're not simply trying to get through the day, but savoring moments of every day.

The Little Pink Book of Elegance is your guide to enhancing your life, one elegant touch at a time. And you'll be surprised. Having the right thing in your closet, for example, *can* actually save you time and money. But elegance is much more than what you wear. It's about managing all aspects of your life with poise and self-confidence, and refining your own true-to-yourself style. Elegant inspiration is everywhere. Movies, fashion, even architecture can be the catalyst for adding grace and beauty to your home, wardrobe, and daily interactions. So pour yourself a cup of coffee—in a real cup—and relax for a moment or two. Elegance is just a rich, delicious sip away.

what is elegance?

The only real elegance is in the mind;
If you've got that, the rest really comes from it.

<small>DIANA VREELAND</small>

MODERN ELEGANCE

Think elegance, and you automatically picture 1940s movie stars and society women who lunch. So where and how does elegance fit into our modern lives? What is elegance, and how do you get it?

The word elegance is derived from the Latin *eligere,* meaning *to select.* Elegance, then, is something that can be cultivated. It has to do with the choices you make and how you put things (including yourself!) together. And when you think about it, choice is one of the things that makes elegance completely relevant in this day and age. We certainly have a plethora of choices about everything, from the brand of jeans we wear to the shows

 we watch on television. And yet, with all this choice, there is a trend toward sameness, toward fitting in, toward looking and living like everyone

else. Elegance is about refining those choices to reflect your own unique, personal style. Modern elegance is about being authentic.

Living elegantly must be achieved through experience. Teenagers are often enchanted with the latest fashion or trend, but they are rarely elegant. Elegance connotes a certain sophistication, and the self-confidence to make those choices in the first place.

Okay. Elegance is about choice, but it is also about making *certain* choices. We would all probably agree that wearing a tube top to a black tie event is most likely not an elegant choice, although a choice, nonetheless. So how and what do you choose? Where do you begin?

ELEGANT INSPIRATION

Although true elegance emanates from inside, elegance and beauty are all around us, and serve as wonderful teachers. Training your eye to notice beauty in others and in the world outside will help you focus on what you like and want for yourself. True creativity, after all, is really about taking a little of this, and a little of that, and whipping it up into something special that you can call your own. In other words, the world is your oyster, girlfriend—go pry it open! Take notice of other people, art, books, movies, nature, and let the beauty you find be your inspiration. Trust your instincts. You know when you like something, when something you see or experience touches you and makes you appreciate the journey. Get inspired. It's the first step to honing your own sense of style.

Who's Got It?
Elegant Icons

Although it may be hard to accurately define elegance, we all know it when we see it. On the next page is a chart of elegant icons that simply exude IT. Practice fine-tuning your observation skills by matching each icon of elegance with the person, place, or thing with which it is associated. See the answers at the bottom of page 14.

Elegant Icon Quiz

1. Turned up collars

2. Triple strand of pearls

3. Double wrapped tie knot

4. Classic elegance in an Art Deco bottle

5. Gold and diamond "name" necklace

6. Hermès "Kelly" Bag

7. Stainless steel spire, sunbursts and triangular windows

A. Princess Grace

B. The Duke of Windsor

C. Katharine Hepburn

D. Sarah Jessica Parker as Carrie Bradshaw in Sex and the City

E. The Chrysler Building in New York City

F. Jackie O

G. Chanel No. 5

Answers: 1-C, 2-F, 3-B, 4-G, 5-D, 6-A, 7-E

HOW TO GET IT

There are those rare few who are blessed with innate elegance (like the icons mentioned previously) but luckily for the rest of us, elegance, style, and a chic flair are things that can be developed and acquired (and sometimes purchased on eBay!). Here's how to begin:

STEP 1: SIZE YOURSELF UP.

Look at the good, the bad, and the really bad. True elegance begins with honesty, and half the battle is already won once you admit that you aren't perfect. In addition, imperfections are often what make a person stand out among the ordinary. Oscar winner Cate Blanchett, for example, an un-usually elegant modern actress, was told early on that she would-n't make it in the movies—good for theater, maybe—because,

 critics claimed, her nose was too big and her eyes were too small for the silver screen. Her authenticity won out, and has made her an enigmatic star.

STEP 2: MAKE YOUR OWN CHIC LIST.

Once you've looked yourself over, make a list of areas you'd like to focus on, such as wardrobe, home, or interactions with others. Come up with examples of people who seem to pull it off. You'll realize that elegance is attainable, and comes in all different shapes and sizes: classic, refined, relaxed, modern, even slightly tattered.

STEP 3: FAKE IT.

One of the best ways to acquire elegance is to try some on for size. Audrey Hepburn, for example, claimed she didn't rely on any particular acting technique, but found that the clothes she wore were immensely important to conveying a character. She said it was "often an enormous help to know that you looked the part. Then the rest wasn't so tough anymore." In the same vein, trying on a new look or attitude can actually help you attain your goals. If you imagine where you want to go, you stand a much better chance of getting there.

IT'S ALL IN YOUR HEAD

 Elegance is, above all else, a state of mind. It has everything to do with self-awareness and self-confidence. That's why a woman can be "beautiful" by popular standards—fashionable, or textbook attractive—and not be elegant. Some of the most elegant role models, like Coco Chanel or Maya Angelou, may not be described as classic beauties. But they embody undeniable grace and style. So in the end, although you can take your inspiration from others, be true to yourself. Don't give in to someone else's idea of style or beauty. Figure out what YOU want and like, and keep that as your compass. True elegance and style come from honestly expressing yourself.

Of course, everyone can use some guidelines! Read on . . .

wardrobe rules

Clothes make the man.
Naked people have little or
no influence in society.

MARK TWAIN

Dressing elegantly requires more than simply matching the right bag with the right pair of shoes, but stocking your wardrobe with a few essentials will definitely give you a head start. (And will also save you time and hard-earned dollars.) Think about it. How many times have you scrambled around at the last minute, spending whatever you have to on something to wear for a dressy evening out or other special occasion? Here's all you'll need to look like a million, even though you've spent a lot less.

The Ten Items Every Woman Should Have in Her Closet

1. Jeans

Jeans, elegant? Absolutely. Jeans are a modern day staple—as basic to the elegant woman's wardrobe as any little black dress. So put in a little time to find a pair that fits and *flatters* you. (And when you find that pair, buy at least two!) Darker denim will give you more versatility and can easily be dressed up with a cashmere sweater or jacket. Choose jeans with a small amount of spandex in them for a better fit.

Other tricks: a slight flare at the bottom will help balance wide hips or thighs, and is also a good choice when wearing heels.

2. T-shirts

Like jeans, T-shirts have become indispensable

 to the modern wardrobe. Fit is everything. One that is too loose will look matronly. One that is too tight is déclassé. And don't be shy about color; a hint of fuchsia or orange worn under a sweater or jacket can add a simple flair to your basics.

3. WHITE FITTED OR WRAPPED BLOUSE

Every gal needs a great white shirt. The good news: you don't have to spend a bundle. Find one that tapers in at the waist for a sleek silhouette. Or choose one with a crisp collar, worn un-tucked, à la Audrey Hepburn, for a chic, casual look. For instant elegance, try a classic French cuff dress shirt; the required cuff links lend built-in style.

4. SWEATERS, INCLUDING A BLACK TURTLENECK, AND SOMETHING CASHMERE

Sweaters and cardigans have always been a part of the elegant woman's wardrobe. But not all sweaters are created equal. Stick to solid colors (a basic, black turtleneck is a fashion must), and pay attention to the fabric. Silk or cashmere sweaters cost a little more, but will hold up a lot longer than other wools or cottons. And besides, cashmere just makes you *feel* elegant.

5. FABULOUS JACKET OR BLAZER

A short tweed jacket, paired with just about any bottom, is easy chic. Adding one dressy jacket or blazer to your wardrobe will help finish off any outfit. Jackets are also notoriously slimming, especially those that dart in a little at the waist. For a unique look, search for interesting fabrics, or a vintage find.

6. BLACK PANTS

Find at least one pair of classy "dress" pants. Try black gabardine, wool crepe, or a blend of wool and spandex. Black pants are the true workhorse in a modern girl's closet, and can be worn with just about anything else in your wardrobe. Buy a pair that fits comfortably, without any pulls or bulges; pants that are too tight are an elegant disaster.

7. SLEEK KHAKIS

Ever since Diane Keaton wore a pair of baggy men's khakis in the movie, *Annie Hall,* these lightweight, light colored cotton pants have become wardrobe mainstays. When striving for an elegant look, stay away from pleats and sloppy fit. Opt for a sleek pair with a flat front. Legs can be capri length or longer; either choice is elegant as long as it is worn with the right shoes.

8. SKIRT OR DAY DRESS

Katharine Hepburn made it okay for a

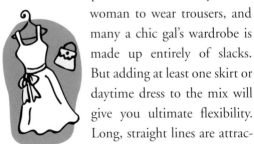

woman to wear trousers, and many a chic gal's wardrobe is made up entirely of slacks. But adding at least one skirt or daytime dress to the mix will give you ultimate flexibility. Long, straight lines are attractive on taller women. Look for a slight flare if you're more full-figured. A simple shift is always in style.

9. SUIT

A tailored, classy suit can be worn for work, dressed up at night, or mixed and matched with your other basics. The fabric is less important than the fit, and as far as color goes, choose black or gray—they will take you the farthest. A fine suit, chosen for quality and enduring style, can last up to five years, so if you have to spend a little more, it'll certainly earn its keep.

10. LITTLE BLACK DRESS

Simply indispensable. How to choose one that will get worn again and again? Pick a simple design with one unique element that gives it flair. A silk satin with a woven trim. A classic A-line, with a low cut neck. Sleeveless styles offer utmost versatility. Also, a hem just at the knee is universally flattering.

UNDER WRAPS: ELEGANT LINGERIE

Too many of us spend too little time on this small, but very important, part of our wardrobes. Simply put, what you wear underneath your clothes is as important as, if not more important than, what you don on the outside. Why? Because fine, well-fitting undergarments will make you feel and look your best.

Women were wearing underthings as early as 3000 B.C.E. (An image of a Sumerian girl from this era, wearing makeshift panties fashioned from a knotted piece of cloth, is on view at the Louvre.) But it was the Victorians, several centuries later, who started really paying attention to what women wore underneath their skirts. In the late 1800s, the Victorians (known ironically for their strict moral codes), "invented" silk panties, which have ever since been associated with upper-class refinement. (The lower classes were unable to afford such fine fabrics, and wore underwear made from rough cotton and muslin.) It  was also the Victorians who appropriated the French word *lingerie* to describe these new, luxurious unmentionables.

Nowadays, most women concern themselves with two main pieces of lingerie: a bra and panties. And when it comes to making an elegant selection, there are only two rules: match the top to the bottom—in color, fabric, and style—and find the proper fit. Wearing a black bra with white underwear, or vice versa, is sloppy (or a sign that your laundry is undone!). The overall color you wear is truly a matter of personal taste, but if in doubt, stick with matching neutrals: white, black, champagne or nude. Silk lingerie is nice, but not always practical.

Cotton and microfiber can also be chic, as long as you wash them properly and get rid of any dingy items.

Now for fit. According to one statistic, 70 percent of all women are wearing the wrong size bra, which doesn't bode well for how the clothes we wear over that bra look! In addition, there is nothing that can derail an otherwise elegant silhouette faster than bulging panty lines. And finally, it's important to feel comfortable in order to look refined, which is eminently harder to pull off if you have a broken underwire jutting into your ribcage. The bottom line: give some thought to your undies—they are truly the foundation of an elegant wardrobe.

COVER STORY: COATS, JACKETS, SHAWLS

Many an elegant look is spoiled by throwing on a coat or wrap that is anything but. It's an easy mistake to make, since it often feels like a Herculean task to get dressed up in the first place. But if you think about the most elegant women you know, or those in the public eye, you'll probably realize they have fabulous outerwear. In the '60s, Jacqueline Kennedy asked her designer of the day, Oleg Cassini, to pay special attention to what she wore over her clothes since she was always being photographed coming and going. Even if you don't have to worry about getting your picture snapped around every corner, a few great coats will transform

almost any ensemble. Here's what you need:

A WINTER COAT

Light colored wools and sumptuous fabrics are often the most chic. It's surprisingly hard to find an elegant black winter coat unless you spend a lot. So go for some color and contrast—you'll wow them.

AN IN-BETWEEN COAT

This can be shorter than your winter coat. Have some fun with fabrics—tweeds, herringbone, corduroy or even velvet. Look for good, simple lines.

A CLASSIC TRENCH

Think Ingrid Bergman in *Casablanca.* A trench adds glamour and style to whatever (or whomever) it covers, and can double as a raincoat. Classic tan is a sure bet, but a pale blue or gray is chic too.

A DRESSY COVER UP, SUCH AS A SILK JACKET, CASHMERE WRAP, PASHMINA, OR STOLE

Whether you think you'll ever need it or not, you will! You simply can't count on the weather or a perfect parking place to assure you can travel without a wrap. Stoles have come back in fashion, and are a fun choice for nighttime glamour. But a cashmere wrap will work overtime. Use it to cover up for a black tie, or throw it around your shoulders, over a turtleneck and jeans.

Note: There will be times when no matter how many other elegant choices you have, nothing but a warm parka will do. It's possible to find one that is both cozy and classy. Steer clear of over-sized numbers that make you look like the Michelin Tire man.

COLOR ME CHIC: BEYOND BASIC BLACK

Remember the trend of assigning a personal color palette based on the seasons? You were an "Autumn," for example, if your skin, hair, and eye tones were in hues that resembled the fall foliage. Choosing certain specific colors, and avoiding others, was said to be the most flattering. The truth is, with a few exceptions, most women can wear any color they want. You might have to adjust your lipstick or accessories, but don't cut yourself off from a certain color just because someone told you once that you could never wear orange! Follow these basic guidelines, then feel free to experiment:

BASIC BLACK

It's true, black is flattering and chic on almost everyone. But dark-haired women, with dark or sallow skin, may need a touch of color with their black to keep from looking washed out. And a wardrobe consisting mostly of black is somewhere between dull and morose. Wear black where it matters—around hips and thighs—and liven up with color elsewhere.

IN THE RED

Red is a good choice for most people (unless you're lucky enough to be a redhead!). When wearing red, don't overdo it. A red dress, red lipstick AND red shoes is too much.

SOFT GRAY AND LIGHT BLUE

These colors look good on almost everyone. Consider them "neutrals."

Trust your instincts and your mirror. It's important to pay attention to what colors do for you. Just don't get in a rut. Life is too short to be stuck in neutral.

COLORS THAT WILL WIDEN YOU:
Light, bright colors like white,
yellow, orange, and lime green

COLORS THAT WILL CAMOUFLAGE YOU:
Beige, grays, pastels

COLORS THAT WILL MINIMIZE YOU:
Blacks, browns, navies

Pretty in Pink

Pink, the "new black," swept onto the scene in 2003, owing its origins not to high-end couture houses, but rather to the Gap and its wildly popular $78 pink raincoat.

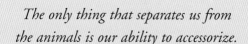

accessorize, accessorize, accessorize!

The only thing that separates us from the animals is our ability to accessorize.

SPOKEN BY OLYMPIA DUKAKIS
AS CLAIREE BELCHER IN *STEEL MAGNOLIAS*

SOLE SISTERS: HOW TO CHOOSE YOUR SHOES

> *The average American woman owns 30 pairs of shoes.*

 Few aspects of a woman's wardrobe excite more lively conversation than when the topic turns to shoes. Everyone from psychologists to archeologists has studied shoes, and their symbolic meaning and relevance. But for most of us, the love of shoes is less cerebral, and more instinctual. Sarah Jessica Parker's character in *Sex and the City* was so wildly addicted to footwear, even her answering machine message paid them tribute: "Hi. I'm not here but my shoes are, so leave them a message." Whether you're an average collector, or a fanatic about your

feet, here's what you need to make your shoe wardrobe a step above:

The Basics

BLACK LEATHER PUMPS—They're the go-to favorite for every outfit in your closet. Dress them up or down; black pumps will always add polish.

METALLIC, HIGH-HEELED SANDALS—A gold or silver strappy sandal can act as an evening neutral. You'll automatically feel and look glamourous.

FLATS OR BALLET SLIPPERS—Choose one with a small heel (an inch or so). It will be more flattering, and still comfortable.

BOOTS—Choose a dressier pair that you can wear with skirts or pants. Pay attention to where the boot hits your calf. One that hits midway

will call attention to the width of your legs.

NEUTRAL SLING BACKS—A pointed, rather than rounded, toe will give you a more refined look.

What Not to Wear

WHITE SHOES—They are, for some reason, never very elegant (unless you're a bride, or a child under 12 years old!).

ANKLE STRAPS—These skinny straps often verge on tacky.

HEELS THAT ARE TOO HIGH—They wreck your posture, and can make you look, well, trashy.

CHUNKY SHOES AND HEELS—They may be

groovy, but they're not elegant.

SHOES WITH TOES THAT CURL UP—Two words: court jester

Head Over Heels

Getting your first pair of high heels is a rite of passage. Heels, after all, are what elevate a plain slipper to a sensuous shoe. Heels have been around for ages, but made their way into fashion in the 1500s when the tiny Catherine de Médicis wore a pair to raise her stature at her marriage to the duc d'Orléans. Afterward, heels became instantly in vogue. Most women have at least one pair in their closet, worn when practical, sensible shoes simply won't do.

Elegant Heels

The Louis

The Kitten

The Cuban

The Prism

The Stiletto

HAVING A HANDLE ON THE SITUATION: THE PERFECT PURSE

Bad feet may prevent you from wearing the latest couture shoes, and a full figure or age may limit your wardrobe choices. But everyone can carry a great bag—and in so doing, can look chic. The reverse is also true. The wrong purse can wreak havoc on an otherwise flawless outfit. So what's an elegant girl to do? Don't worry, the answer is in the bag!

Size Matters

Believe it or not, bigger isn't always better. If you're a petite woman, lugging around a huge bag just looks silly. And no matter how cute that little clutch is, if you can't fit your things in without it bulging open, you should pass. Here's a brief list of the bags (and sizes) you can't live without:

- EVERYDAY BAG—Larger than a lunch box, smaller than a bread box

- EVENING BAG—So many to choose from! Try a satin clutch or a smart satchel made in a luxurious fabric.

- A SUMMER PURSE—Straw, canvas, even patent leather will work.

Extras.

IF YOU CAN SWING IT

- A larger, tailored bag for travel

- A dressy medium-size purse that can be worn in the afternoon or evening

- A stylish work bag (time to give that shopping bag a rest!)

Fine craftsmanship counts when you're shopping for a bag. A classic, well-made bag is worth emptying your purse for. A fine bag can literally last a lifetime.

To prove the point, you can find some great buys and styles when you pick up a vintage bag. Look for them at thrift stores, vintage clothing stores, consignment shops, and even online. (eBay regularly sells used name-brand bags, like Hermès and Prada.) Look for alligator or crocodile skin bags in good condition, with sturdy, structured leather handles. Avoid anything that's frayed, including the inside lining.

ALL TIED UP: SCARVES AND SASHES

 Scarves are among the most versatile of accessories, and can take you from the beach to the boardroom. Here are just a few of the different uses for a scarf:

- Head cover for a bad hair day

- Can't find your belt? Use a colorful sash instead.

- The ultimate beach cover-up: fold a large rectangular scarf in a triangle. Wrap around your waist and tie a knot on the side for a stylish sarong.

- Tie a sash or scarf around the brim of a straw hat to add color and flair.

- Drape a large scarf around your shoulders for an elegant black-tie cover-up.

● Wear as a headband, like Liz Taylor in *Suddenly Last Summer,* for casual elegance.

How to Tie a Scarf with Style

If you've ever been to Paris, you know the women there just seem to have a knack for tying the ultimate chic scarf. To achieve an elegant look, designer Nicole Miller offers the following advice:

"For a Parisian look, use a square scarf. Fold it into a triangle and then roll the long side toward the short side until it becomes ropelike. Then wrap it around your neck with a chic knot on the side."

For an elegant look with an oblong scarf: fold it in half, and secure it around your neck by looping the two scarf ends through the other folded end. Cinch it around your neck and

wear it over a turtleneck or under a jacket to keep yourself warm.

Accidental Elegance

Style icon Babe Paley showed up for lunch at La Grenouille with a scarf tied to her handbag, and voilà, an instant new fashion was born!

HEAD FIRST:
HATS AND GLOVES

Hats and gloves used to be non-negotiable—the proper finishing touch to any elegant outfit. But since the 1960s, hats and gloves have shifted from necessities to true accessories.

Gloves in a wide array of colors and with pretty trims can add sparkle and a touch of humor to an otherwise traditional look. Never wear gloves indoors, unless you're wearing them at a formal event, such as the opera, and never when you're eating. Speaking of gloves, rubber ones are worth the investment. There's no better way to keep your hands from getting chapped and worn when you're cleaning or doing dishes.

And hats . . . well, some gals were just born to wear hats. You know who you are! When shopping for a hat, try it on when your hair isn't perfect. If it looks good with undone hair, you'll be extremely pleased when your hair is coiffed. The array of hat choices will make your head spin.

To test your hat IQ.

TAKE THE QUIZ BELOW:

1. WHICH OF THE FOLLOWING IS NOT AN ACTUAL HAT STYLE?

   a. Pillbox   d. Toque
   b. Lampshade   e. Cloche
   c. Boggle

2. WHICH ARBITER OF STYLE STARTED HER CAREER AS A MILLINER?

   a. Coco Chanel   c. Donna Karan
   b. Diana Vreeland   d. Kate Spade

3. FAYE DUNAWAY GAVE THE BERET NEW FASHION IMPORTANCE WHEN SHE WORE IT IN WHAT MOVIE?

a. The Great Gatsby
b. Bonnie and Clyde
c. The Thomas Crown Affair
d. Chinatown

4. FRENCH DESIGNER ELSA SCHIAPARELLI WAS KNOWN FOR HER AVANT-GARDE DESIGNS, INCLUDING HER FAMOUS BIRD'S NEST AND LAMB CHOP HATS. WHAT COLOR WERE THE HAT BOXES SHE PUT THEM IN?

a. robin's egg blue   c. tangerine
b. shocking pink   d. chartreuse

Answers: 1-c, 2-a, 3-b, 4-b

all that glitters

*The rarest things in the world,
next to a spirit of discernment,
are diamonds and pearls.*

JEAN DE LA BRUYÈRE

THE RULES ON JEWELS

There's nothing like jewelry to cheer a girl up when she's got the blues (or, for that matter, the "reds," as was the case with Holly Golightly in *Breakfast at Tiffany's*).

Besides having a calming effect, jewelry is also one of the simplest ways to assert your own personal style. The rules on jewels have changed over the years: for example, it was once considered gauche to wear dangly earrings in the daytime, and diamonds were reserved for women 30 years or older. While simplicity is still the elegant woman's watchword, it should not be exercised at the expense of personal expression. In other words, have fun with your jewels; just don't overdo it.

So how much is too much? When you're getting

dressed, adorn yourself with your favorite baubles, then see if you can remove one piece. Don't overload yourself with a necklace, earrings, pin, AND bracelet. It is much more chic to wear an armful of bangles, and nothing else. Or only earrings and a great brooch (very much in style these days). Jewelry should make you sparkle, but should not, in and of itself, be the star.

Most important, wear what you like. If you have a favorite piece of jewelry, don't be afraid to wear it all the time. Give an heirloom or other meaningful piece special consideration. Jewelry which reminds you of someone or something special can act like an amulet, readying you for a new situation (like a job interview), making you feel lucky or protected. So if your grandmother's pearls make you smile, don't be afraid to wear them with a cashmere sweater and jeans. Have confidence—it will shine through.

PEARLY GREATS

Speaking of pearls . . . pearls and elegance are practically synonymous. No other single accessory is more closely identified with elegance than a strand (or two, or seven) of pearls. And no matter if they are real or faux, just as long as they are strung properly (with small knots in between each pearl) and worn often. In fact, if real pearls *aren't* worn often, they'll lose their luster.

A strand of big pearls or small pearls is especially elegant. But you can lose those pearl earrings trimmed in gold dating back to the '80s—they're a little frumpy. Wear your pearls with a sleeveless silk T-shirt, or to a black-tie event. Babe Paley wore hers wrapped around her wrists, forming a cascade of pearl "bracelets" which she mixed with other bangles and gems

for a signature look. No matter how you slice it (or how your wear them), pearls are a must.

Tips on Caring for Pearls

- Store pearls separately in a jewelry bag to avoid scratches.

- Do not "wash" pearls with jewelry cleaner or soap and water. Simply wipe them clean with a soft cloth after you wear them.

- Apply hairspray and perfume BEFORE you put on your pearls, as they may dull the pearls or harm them.

CHARMED, I'M SURE

A few words about this timeless accoutrement—the charm bracelet. These jangly, lovely baubles are as much fun to wear as they are to look at, and have been around since the 1920s and '30s. They may represent the ultimate "personal" jewelry, as charms often tell a story or commemorate special events. When designers like Elsa Schiaparelli and Coco Chanel came out with their own unique versions in the '40s, style icons and celebrities soon took notice. In 1944, Lauren Bacall was photographed with hers in *Harper's Bazaar,* and Jackie O often wore one, featuring a single, large charm dangling from a gold link chain.

Charm bracelets waned in popularity in the 1960s and '70s, but have found a following again, thanks in part to Sarah Jessica Parker and her

onscreen persona, Carrie Bradshaw. ("Both" gals took a shine to them.) So dust off your mother's keepsake bracelet, or go buy one of your own. The results are sure to be nothing less than charming.

DIAMOND JUBILATION

Diamonds are the icing on (or in) any gal's jewelry box. It's hard to describe what makes them so alluring. But if you're lucky enough to be in the market for one or more, here are a few things to remember.

● A beautiful diamond is not only a fine addition to your jewelry collection; it's an investment. Set your budget, then balance quality with appearance. Remember, a stone does not have to be perfect to be valuable (or enjoyable). Just make sure you're an educated consumer, so you get your money's worth.

- Quality comes down to knowing the four C's: cut, clarity, color, carats. Each one of these impacts the value and price of a diamond. To learn more about buying a diamond, consult a reputable website, such  as www.thediamondbuyingguide.com, and shop at a jewelry store you can trust.

- Make sure your diamond is certified and appraised before you buy it. Look for a GIA or EGL certified stone.

Once You Own a Diamond.

KEEP THE FOLLOWING TIPS IN MIND:

- Consider lasering your girdle. No, we're not talking undergarments here. Nowadays, you can get an "ID" number inscribed on the girdle (the widest part) of your diamond for identification purposes. This number (visible only through a jeweler's loupe) can protect you when you get your ring repaired.

⬤ "Keep it clean, honey." A diamond may be forever, but that doesn't mean it looks good covered with soap scum or cookie dough.

⬤ Most important, wear your diamonds and enjoy them. They are indeed the hardest substance on earth, and, therefore, the stones themselves are very durable. (Check settings from time to time, however, as prongs can loosen or break.)

FAKING IT: WHEN CUBIC ZIRCONIA WILL DO

There are several schools of thought on fake jewels. Regarding cubic zirconia, adherents of old school elegance look down on fake diamonds, warning that trying to pull off a fake will make you look like a fraud. But if chosen with care, and for the right effect, cubic zirconia can come in very handy, thank you. Take "diamond" studs. Maybe Oprah can splurge on the real ones, but there's no need for the rest of us to break the bank. The key is buying a pair that isn't too big, and, therefore, clearly fake. Simply attach to earlobes, and enjoy!

Other more obvious costume jewelry (including ornate rhinestones) also has its place. The secret is to wear costume pieces for what they are: a fun way to add personality to your wardrobe. Just remember the following:

- White beads are best worn in the summer, if at all.

- Avoid gobs and gobs of costume glitter—you'll look like you just got back from Mardi Gras.

- Don't be afraid to mix the fakes with the real stuff—variety is the spice of life.

- Costume jewelry is often more delicate than the real thing. Keep water away. It can loosen adhesives and corrode finishes.

- Perfumes can "attach" to costume jewelry. Wait a few minutes to let fragrances set before you put on your gems.

Accidental Elegance

Jackie O was famous for the three-strand pearl necklace she wore throughout her life—the very picture of elegance. But when the pearls were auctioned off at Sotheby's in 1996, we learned they were simulated. In other words, fake!

bare elegance

What is elegance? Soap and water!

<small>CECIL BEATON</small>

L et's face it. You can't be elegant if you're a mess. Seems obvious, but how many times have you seen someone who's wearing all the right clothes, the perfect hairdo, or the most chic accessories and who still comes across as less than elegant? A closer look will probably reveal that the discrepancy lies with grooming. Good grooming is about two things: cleanliness and taking good care of things (your body and your clothes).

Because the demands of our daily lives are so hectic, taking good care of ourselves often comes last. And like so many other things, once you get behind on grooming, it often takes a lot more time and money to fix what you've left undone. Even so, this argument is still not enough to encourage some very busy, tired women to put themselves first.

CLEANLINESS IS NEXT TO GODLINESS

 While certain hygiene routines should go without saying, you'd be surprised how often we trip ourselves up by doing one or many of the following:

- Not removing makeup at night.

- Not keeping nails well groomed and hands, elbows, feet, and knees moisturized.

- Not flossing!

- Not keeping up with hair removal (tweezing, shaving, waxing, etc.).

- Convincing yourself that washing your hair, or yourself, too often is drying, and therefore risking a less than fresh odor!

If taking care of yourself has fallen to the bottom of your priority list, it's time to bump yourself back to the top. To keep from feeling overwhelmed, focus your efforts by picking just one area you'd like to improve, and making *one* change that will help you achieve this. For example: put a bottle of lotion in a pretty container by your bed or next to the kitchen sink so you don't have to remember to moisturize. Or make a special manicure date with your friend or daughter, so you can tend to your nails while also spending time together. Make taking care of yourself a no-brainer, and you just might do it.

WARDROBE MAINTENANCE

Check for the following before you leave the house:

- A fallen hemline (or one that's held up by tape or safety pins) is elegance undone. To avoid a last minute scramble, check your pants AFTER you wear them, and BEFORE you put them away.

- Shoes should be in good condition. That means clean, polished, and heels free of mud. Repair dingy shoes or toss them out.

- Pay attention to linings. Ripped or loose linings make you look like a wreck.

- Bra straps. They should be clean, untangled, and preferably not showing.

- Clothes should be free of spots, dirt, crumbs and odors. If you can see it or smell it, so can everyone else!

- Trim pilling sweaters and wool jackets so they don't look like your dog just finished sleeping on them.

- Introduce yourself to your iron. Press your clothes after you wash them and before you put them away. If you can't stand to iron, take clothes to the laundry to be pressed; you can't look crisp and clean if your clothes aren't.

HAIR MAINTENANCE

Good hair (and a good haircut) are the best accessories you can have. After all, what other article of clothing or accessory do you wear every day?

Elegant hair is healthy hair. It's shiny, clean, bouncy, and dandruff free. Hair is one of the first places that will show poor nutrition, stress, and so on. So take care of your hair by eating right and exercising. (Hair is nourished by detoxified blood and plenty of nutrients.) Use gentle cleansers and conditioners, and as few chemicals as you can. Natural, "old fashioned" treatments also work well: rinsing with a little lemon juice or vinegar will remove soap buildup and help restore shine. Mixing an egg in with your shampoo can help strengthen hair.

Mostly, make sure your hair looks real—soft, clean, and alive. Too much hairspray, extreme or severe styles, and unnatural colors are roadblocks to elegance.

Splurging on a Great Do

Much has been written about designer haircuts, with price tags that rival monthly car payments! But these extremes aside, spending a little more on a good haircut will pay you back in spades. A good cut will keep you from fighting with your hair on a daily basis. And what's more, a stylist will often know what flatters you, even if you're unable to glean it yourself.

To Color or Not to Color

This is another matter best left to personal choice. But keep the following things in mind before you run head first to your colorist: it's not a crime to go gray, and light hair is often ultimately more flattering on older women than

severe or unnatural colors. The trick to making the most of your gray is to dress the rest of yourself accordingly. Tweak your makeup, hairstyle, and clothes toward dramatic and gorgeous. There is nothing that says "confidence" more than a woman who's gone gray and played it up to her advantage.

If gray is just not your bag, think soft and subtle, and avoid extremes in color or striped highlights. A color that is harsh or too dark is actually spookier than a little gray. And once you start coloring your hair, keep on top of it. Two-tone hair is hard to pull off unless you're a zebra.

YOU CAN TELL A LADY
BY HER HANDS

Remember the scene in *Gone with the Wind,* when Scarlett goes to visit Rhett, dressed in an outfit she's concocted from a pair of old drapes? Rhett is impressed with her finery at first, but discovers her charade when he takes her hands in his. Scarlett's rough, worn skin gives her away.

Ragged hands and nails are undeniably detrimental to good looks. But you don't have to spend a fortune (in time and money) on weekly manicures to resolve the problem. Just keep the following basics in mind: keep your hands and nails clean; push back your cuticles (which you can do gently every time you wash your hands); keep nails trimmed and filed (do this while you're watching TV or

before you shower); and keep your hands, wrists, and elbows moisturized.

Regarding polish, bright colors look especially good on women with well-shaped hands and nails. Otherwise stick to very pale shades with a little luster, to emphasize that your nails are clean. Although polish definitely adds just that, if you're not good about changing or fixing your polish, it's better to wear none at all.

FACE FACTS

The first thing you have to remember about your face is that you don't have to have perfect features to exude perfect beauty.  Really. Beauty, which we often notice first in someone's face, is about an inner glow that shines through our features. It's radiance in the true sense of the word. Furthermore, the most beautiful women in the world usually have some feature that's out of sync, allowing them to be unique. So, as the song says: accentuate the positive.

To help illuminate your inner beauty, make sure your skin is in healthy shape by following these skin care basics:

- Eat right, drink enough water, and get plenty of sleep. The older you get, the more you'll be convinced of this timeless beauty maxim.

- Cover up and protect yourself from the sun. Not only is leathery, over-tanned skin inelegant, it's unhealthy. Use a face and body moisturizer with a built-in sunscreen of at least 15 SPF, and wear a wide-brimmed hat to help protect your face. It has the added advantage of looking quite chic.

- Invest in a good cleanser, moisturizer, and eye cream, and leave that bar of deodorant soap in the shower where it belongs.

- Stop smoking and drinking in excess. Both will dehydrate your skin and add years to your looks.

- Stop picking! We've all done it, and then regretted it. Leave pimples and blackheads to the experts.

MAKEUP DOS AND DON'TS

Once you've prepped your skin, you can turn your attention to makeup. Although some women can get by with very little or none at all (like style icon C.Z. Guest, who relied on the simplest of make-up to accentuate her regal beauty), most women can benefit from at least a little touch, here and there.

Basic Tools
AND WHAT NOT TO DO WITH THEM

1. LIPSTICK

Many consider it their essential makeup product. Just make sure to avoid: severe colors that look unnatural; lining your lips larger than they really are (you'll look "made-up"); and neglecting to

coordinate your shade of lipstick with your clothes.

2. EYE SHADOW

If you MUST wear green or blue eye shadow, wear it only at night. Otherwise stick to more muted colors that will put the emphasis on your eyes, not your eyelids.

3. FOUNDATION

Don't be afraid! Just make sure to find one that matches your own coloring (many makeup artists recommend a yellow toned base as flattering), and try it out for yourself. Don't let a salesperson talk you into something.

4. EYELINER AND MASCARA

Never apply liner to the inside of your eyelids. It can cause infection, and will actually make your eyes look smaller. Black and brown-black mascaras look the most natural. (Blue, purple, and red mascaras are hard to pull off.) Avoid clumping by using a thinner mascara.

5. BLUSH

There are all sorts of rules about blush. Stick to this one: make it look natural. Forget about "building" cheekbones; add light color where you'd really see it if you were blushing.

Finally:

Blend, Blend, Blend! As one friend put it, unblended makeup makes you look a little crazy. Apply and reapply your makeup at home or in the ladies room. Putting it on in public is not classy. And last, once you have your makeup on, forget about it. Constantly worrying about your makeup calls attention to it.

scentsations

*No elegance is possible
without perfume.*

COCO CHANEL

PERFUME THROUGH THE AGES

Fragrance, and its ability to conjure up certain moods, emotions, and memories, is one of the most intriguing aspects of fashion—and one of the oldest.

Scents have been prized as long as history has been recorded. As early as 2000 B.C.E., smoke from sweet-smelling woods and other incense was used in all sorts of Egyptian rituals, including embalmings. In fact, *perfume* comes from the Latin words *per,* meaning "through," and *fumus,* which means "smoke."

Fragrant body scents and lotions came later, and were made from flowers, herbs, and spices mixed with animal fats and vegetable oils. Perfumes and other scents have been

 used throughout history to attract, entice, heal, and celebrate. Cleopatra is said to have saturated the sails of her ship with her perfume so that Mark Antony would crave her when he sailed into her port. Scents have also been used, not surprisingly, to cover up other, less pleasant odors, as was the case in 17th century France, when daily hygiene rituals left much to be desired.

One of the most interesting characteristics of perfume, of course, is how it makes the wearer feel, and how it imprints itself on others. For these reasons, perfume is one of the strongest tools a woman has at her disposal— an ally that can do more for her mood and her general demeanor than a closet full of designer clothes.

Traditionally, women were inclined to pick one perfume, and remained faithful to that scent without straying. But nowadays, women are more open to choosing different fragrances for various occasions or moods, and adding variety by using scented soaps, lotions and bath gels.

No matter if you're in the market for one or several fragrances, the only way to find your perfect fit is through trial and error. When shopping for perfume, take a sample whiff by spraying some onto a paper perfume blotter. That way you can get an idea of what you like before you confuse yourself with too many smells.

The longest lasting scents are found in perfumes, which contain a higher concentration of essential oils than *eau de parfum* or next, the *eau de toilette*. Cologne has the least amount of concentrated oils and, consequently, lasts the shortest time. No matter which way you go, remember that an elegant woman's perfume should

never upstage her. It should tickle the senses without overwhelming anybody, or leaving a heavy trail behind.

The Sweet Smell of Success

An astrologer told Coco Chanel that five was her lucky number. So she named her first perfume Chanel No. 5 and launched it on the fifth day of May (the fifth month). The rest, as they say, is history.

BURNING DESIRE

Aside from wearable perfume, try scented candles, oils, and room sprays to strike an air of elegance. Below is a brief glossary of fragrances for the home:

CANDLES

Not just for the dinner table anymore! Candles are the most common form of portable fragrance, and can set a mood through aesthetic senses of both sight and smell.

ROOM SPRAYS

These offer instant fragrance, but dissipate quickly. Avoid spraying onto fabrics and carpets; they can leave a lasting scent or stain.

INCENSE

Typically more intense than other room scents, and also more exotic.

Incense sticks have evolved to include name brand perfumes and lighter aromas that are more subtle than traditional incense.

POTPOURRI

This mainstay is made up of dried herbs, flowers, spices, and even dried fruit. Will last around a month, but can also be "refreshed" with additional oil or room sprays.

SACHETS AND SCENTED PAPERS

Used to freshen closets and dresser drawers. The height of elegance is to have your sachets match the scent of your perfume.

ESSENTIAL OILS

These highly concentrated oils are extracted from all sorts of botanicals, including flow-

ers, fruits, roots and trees. Oils are not typically applied directly to the skin. Instead, they are added to other "carrier" oils, diluted in water, or dispersed through heat-activated diffusers.

Many oils are believed to carry therapeutic properties.

STOP AND SMELL THE ROSES

Fresh flowers are one of the simplest ways to incorporate a delicious scent and elegant touch to your surroundings. Certain flowers are automatically associated with specific meanings: a red rose for love; a white lily for sorrow or mourning.

Cutting Flowers

When you go to the trouble of buying or picking flowers, you want them to last. Give store-bought or just picked flowers a fresh cut at an angle while under water before you arrange them. Remove any leaves that will fall under the water line to prevent bacteria

from breeding. Fill your vase with water that is room temperature or warmer, and add floral food. You can also add a few drops of bleach to help reduce bacteria.

Arranging Flowers

The trick to arranging flowers is simplicity. The more simple the arrangement, the more elegant. This does not mean sparse. It means organizing flowers with a pureness in mind. For example, you can arrange a variety of different flowers together as long as you don't mix too many colors. The reverse is also true: a vase of roses or gerber daisies in a rainbow of colors, mixed with nothing else, looks great. If you want to mix flower types, stick to only two colors, otherwise the results will be chaotic. Some of the most dramatic bouquets are large amounts of the same kind of flowers, cut short and bunched together. A cylinder vase brimming with roses, tulips, even carnations, can be elegant as long as there are plenty of them. Single flowers, placed in uniform vases are also very appealing.

And when flowers begin to fade, toss them before they obviously need to be trashed. Don't feel guilty—elegance may be timeless, but beauty is ephemeral.

organizing principles

Less is more.

MIES VAN DER ROHE,
ARCHITECT

CLOSET CASE

An organized closet is one of the best ways to pave a path to elegance. Why? Because if your clothes are easy to get to, stored in good condition, AND in a place that is aesthetically appealing, getting dressed will be a pleasure, and your appearance will reflect that.

But the state of your closet can also influence more than how you dress; it can affect your general well being as well. As any woman knows, a messy closet is like a dirty little secret; it's unsettling, embarrassing, and makes you feel bad.

Okay. We all crave that perfect, moviestar closet, with plenty of room for all of our things. (Oprah's recent closet makeover featured shelves for 192 pairs of shoes!) But let's get real. Most of us

have closets that are too small, clothes that are anything but red carpet worthy, and not a lot of time and money to do anything about it.

Here's the good news: getting to the bottom of a messy closet will take just a few hours (allow between three and six). And you don't have to spend a lot on a fancy, professional "closet system." In fact, before you go out and purchase any organizers or containers, start with the following:

1. SORT

Take everything out of your closet and separate into categories, such as pants, shirts, sweaters, shoes, and so on. This will help you see what you've got—and what you've got too many of. Do you really need, or wear, all seven pairs of black pants?

2. DELETE

Get rid of anything that is tattered, and cannot be easily repaired. (That means items that are broken, have holes, stains, rips, or have become shapeless.) Ditch clothes that don't fit anymore. Chances are, by the time you get back into your "skinny clothes," you'll

want to treat yourself to some new ones. And get rid of things you haven't worn in the last two years.

3. FIND A HOME

"A place for everything, and everything in its place" is an organizer's credo for a reason— it works! You must designate an area for everything you've decided to keep. Go through each category, and map out its home. This is the single most important rule to follow.

4. HOLD EVERYTHING

You'll probably like this part! Armed with proper measurements, gather containers that are both functional and pretty. If your closet functions well and looks great, you are 100 percent more likely to keep it up. Choose attractive, open baskets to store loose items like gym clothes, give-aways, and casual shoes, such as slippers. Store your other shoes on shelves, in shoe bags, on racks, or in shoe boxes that are clearly labeled. Don't "hide" too many things in dark corners or opaque containers. Out of sight means out of mind; you'll forget what you have and where to put it.

5. MAINTENANCE

If you've gotten this far, maintenance won't be hard. The best way to maintain order in your closet is to follow this rule: for each new item, get rid of an old one. It just makes sense. Once you've maxed out your storage, you can't add something new without removing something else, or you'll just be back where you started.

Other Elegant and Useful Touches

- Buy some sturdy valet hooks, and install on your closet door or wall to hang pajamas, belts, purses or clothes that need to be repaired.

- Tie a ribbon on the end of a lint brush or roller, and hang on a hook or door knob for easy access (and easy dog hair removal!).

- Hang up something pretty, personal or inspiring in your closet: a favorite photo, a framed treasured handkerchief, heirloom necklace, or vintage purse. It will add a note of calm. What could be more elegant?

Do not store clothes in dry-cleaner plastic bags. They can trap moisture and solvent fumes inside, and can cause yellow streaks on fabrics. In addition, they will make your closet look less tidy, and collect dust.

A Note About Hangers

Wooden and padded hangers are wonderful, to be sure. But you don't have to fill your closet with them to achieve elegance. These types of hangers take up more space than plastic or wire ones. When going for a sleek look, go for uniformity.

PURGING YOUR PURSE

A woman's purse is her traveling command central, housing her most important and often used tools of the trade. So hav- ing a purse that lightens your daily load (instead of weighing you down) is key.

A bulging bag is a lot of things, but it's not elegant. If keeping your purse clean feels like a Sisyphean task, follow these steps towards redemption:

1. DUMP IT OUT, THEN CLEAN IT OUT

Empty everything out on a table and sort through your stuff. Separate items into:

- Things you use every day (keys, wallet, lipstick, etc.)

- Things you use just once (shopping list, bills to mail, an article to read, etc.)

95

● Junk (this may include scraps of paper, furry Life Savers, or a stray Barbie-doll shoe)

2. CONTAIN YOURSELF

Once again, your best bet is to find a home for everything:

● Keep essentials in separate, zippered pouches, such as makeup in one pouch, and stamps, pen, and paper in another. This will also make switching bags a breeze.

● Match your purse accessories for an elegant, clean look. A wallet, makeup pouch, and notebook made out of the same fabric or color brings order out of chaos. Clear pouches are helpful for keeping things separate but easy to find.

● Clip loose papers such as a shopping list or bills together with a large, colorful paper or binder clip, or fasten with an elastic band around a small notebook. This will help you from losing a stray piece of information.

 Keep your receipts and coupons in a separate, leather envelope or other pouch, to keep your wallet from gaping open.

3. KEEP IT UP

Maintenance always seems to be the hardest part. But look at it this way. Daily upkeep will take only a few minutes. Or make it a weekly ritual and spend about 10 to 15 minutes. Either way, staying on top of your purse will make you feel in control, and less harried. It's one small thing that will have a big impact on a daily basis.

home, elegant home

*Beauty of style and harmony
and grace and good rhythm
depend on simplicity.*

PLATO

IF YOUR WALLS COULD TALK

Clothes may make the man, but what, if anything, does your house say about you? Plenty! In fact, many argue that your home is like a self-portrait revealing a great deal about the *real* you. In one psychological study on the subject, participants who spent only 15 to 20 minutes in a stranger's bedroom did as good a job as the inhabitant's close friends at judging that individual's personality traits. Hard to believe? The ancient Chinese practice of feng shui also promotes this notion: "As within, so without."

And not only are our surroundings emblematic of "who we are"; they can also influence how our lives work. One of the best examples of this is clutter. Clutter literally and figuratively obstructs our lives and

 stifles elegance. Here are a few general suggestions for cutting out clutter so you can see the forest for the trees (or at least the top of your dining room table!):

1. THE SEVEN SECOND RULE

It takes as little as seven seconds to do the following: put everything right back into your medicine cabinet after you use it; load a dish directly into the dishwasher; throw out junk mail the minute it comes in; and put laundry away immediately instead of piling it on your bed. Not convinced? Count for yourself. It often takes less than a minute to finish the job, saving you from a stack of chores that will seem much more overwhelming later on.

2. POSITIVE CHANGE

Collect all your loose change in one place instead of in bowls and cups all over the house. Designate one container, such as a pretty antique jar. When it's full, convert the coins into paper money or donate the change to charity.

3. GIVE IT UP

Set aside a specific area (such as your front hall closet or by the door to your garage) for a give-away basket. Place clothes, kitchen items and books you've finished reading in the basket. When it's full, get rid of the stuff!

4. BABY STEPS

If your clutter is overwhelming, attack one pile a day. Commit to this approach for one week, and see if the results can motivate you to continue.

ROOM BY ROOM

When clutter is at bay, you can concentrate on adding elegant touches to your home, one room at a time.

The Bedroom

Use a single color throughout the room, along with white, to create a retreat that is crisp and serene.

Pay attention to what's on your bed table: too much stuff next to your head can be distracting, and may interfere with a restful night's sleep. Limit items to things that are attractive and useful: a pretty lamp, an artsy alarm clock and so on. Store items like hand creams, lip balms, or the remote control, in a bed table drawer or basket.

Make it personal and warm. If your bedroom is going to say something about you, make sure it says the right thing! Items that are special to you, unique, or simply tickle your fancy will make your house not only elegant, but a true expression of who you are. When displaying your treasures, keep simplicity in mind. A dresser covered with photos, for example, can look like a mess. Better to feature one or two favorites in beautiful frames.

The Bathroom

Add an Oriental flair and touch of elegance by placing an orchid plant or beautiful bowl filled with smooth stones near the sink.

Use an antique silver tray to hold a collection of candles, all in hues of the same color.

Remind yourself of the Ritz by rolling extra bath towels or washcloths instead of folding them. Store them in a wicker or metal basket.

The Living Room

Punctuate subdued colors and rich textures with a touch of gold, such as a gilt framed picture, a golden Buddha, or pillows with some rich detail.

Use velvet—it has the benefit of being both luxurious and surprisingly durable. Like a velvet jacket, accessories made from this lush fabric will dress up your living room. Velvet pillows and throws make a subtle statement. Or use velvet to cover one small piece of furniture, such as an ottoman, for a rich accent.

Mirrors are a wonderful way to add sparkle and light to any space. Consider hanging a few small ones together on one

 wall. Display an antique one on a bookshelf. Or use a grand full-length mirror to enlarge your space. Mirrors should be

framed, or at least have a beveled edge. Use mirrors to reflect light and beauty (not clutter, partial views,

or a window that looks out onto a busy road).

The Dining Room

Choose a centerpiece for your table. An empty table almost invites clutter, so place something substantial in the middle to discourage you from junking up the rest. Fresh flowers are a wonderful choice, but hard to maintain. Consider potted, flowering plants: three small orchids, or a pot of tulips. A large bowl, plate, or antique compote filled with fruit is also pretty. (Artificial flowers and fruit are tricky, and risk looking a little less than elegant.)

Candles also make this room particularly elegant, either on the table or in wall sconces.

Use cloth napkins and silver salt and

pepper shakers. Even if you're dining casually, these items will elevate any meal.

The Kitchen

Lack of clutter (or at least *areas* that are clutter free) is the key to elegance in this workhorse of a room. Only appliances that are used on a daily basis should be left out on the counters (that means your Cuisinart should be put away). Even if you have a small kitchen, try to leave one counter completely clear. It will add serenity to the space.

Unified colors or tones of color are often more elegant than bright, loud shades. That doesn't mean sterile; use color as accents (like a red teapot, flowering plants, pretty bowls or colorful artwork).

Beware of overflowing bulletin boards. That goes for hanging tons of papers on your fridge, too. Try placing corkboards inside a cupboard or pantry door instead.

Or use a chalkboard, which will help achieve a streamlined look.

The Linen Closet

Organize your linens into two categories: bed linens and towels. These items should be separated from each other, and then organized by color, AND by where they belong in the house. Organizing by color will give a visual sense of order.

Put clean towels or sheets on top of the pile, and take the set to be used from the bottom. This way, linens get worn evenly, and the circulation prevents musty, stale odors.

Shelf liners and labels are the height of elegance in a linen closet. They will also help others who are using the closet know where things belong.

elegant entertaining

*One cannot think well, love well,
sleep well, if one has not dined well.*

VIRGINIA WOOLF,
A ROOM OF ONE'S OWN

LIFE OF THE PARTY

What better way to celebrate your newfound elegance (and that little black dress) than by throwing a party? If you're not ready for a formal affair, consider hosting a fabulous cocktail party—it's elegant entertaining, made easy!

Cocktail parties have enjoyed a lively comeback recently, due in part to a renewed interest in both classic and modern mixed drinks. (See The Cosmopolitan recipe on page 114.) In addition, a cocktail party allows you to reciprocate a bundle of invitations in one fell swoop—certainly a plus for the busy, modern gal.

If you find planning a party daunting, don't fret. The art of throwing the perfect cocktail party isn't some mysterious talent. Follow these basic rules to create the right energy,

and make your party a hit whether you've invited 15 or 50!

1. THE GUEST LIST

In large part, it's the people who make the party, so give great thought to your guest list. Mix up ages, geographical locales, and occupations, and invite people you'd like to introduce to one another. It's often helpful to invite an equal number of guys and gals, but for a larger group, the balance is not as important. Try to avoid combustible guests: if you know two people don't get along, invite them on separate evenings.

2. INVITES MATTER

For a small or spur of the moment party, an invite by phone is fine. But for a larger group—say over 15 people—written invitations are the better way to go. You should give people at least one to four weeks notice. Written invitations should specify a set length of time for the party: for example, "6:00 to 9:00." In addition, make sure to mention dress. Is it casual or "cocktail party attire"?

3. STOCK YOUR LIQUOR CABINET

If you're throwing a cocktail party, guests will be disappointed if you are serving only wine and beer. Make sure you have enough of these basics: scotch, bourbon, whiskey, gin, vodka, and rum. Typical mixers include tonic water, soda, cola, ginger ale, and juices, including orange, pineapple, tomato, and cranberry. If you're planning to offer specialty drinks, make sure to have ingredients on hand, such as vermouth and olives for martinis. And of course, for an elegant touch, don't forget the champagne!

4. IT'S ALL IN THE PLANNING

The best way to ensure an elegant success is to plan ahead, so you can be ready in advance of your guests. This is tricky, to be sure, but it's also key. Coming into a party where the hostess is frazzled or spends the whole night working in the kitchen makes guests feel they're an imposition. Plan a menu that you can pull off, and don't attempt complicated hors d'oeuvres that have to be made once the party's underway. Try a tasty bruschetta; grilled shrimp; prosciutto and melon; figs and goat cheese—things your guests can eat with their fingers, assisted by nothing more than a cocktail napkin. Easy additions, like olives, nuts, gourmet cheese and specialty crackers are fine to round out the offerings.

5. GET HELP IF YOU CAN

If you can swing it, invest in a bartender or

serving and cleaning help for the evening. It might sound like an extravagance, but especially with a large party, consider whether you really want to be mixing drinks all night long. Instead, use your talents to make sure guests are comfortable and mingling with each other. The sign of a truly great party is if the hostess also enjoys herself.

6. ROLL WITH THE PUNCHES

Something is bound to go wrong on your big night—it always does—so expect it! But don't let one little blunder, missing ingredient or cancellation wreck your mood. Be gracious and relaxed, even if someone shows up with an uninvited guest or you burn the mini quiches. Laughing at life's curveballs will help you remain graceful and gracious, and this will put your guests at ease.

Elegance with a Twist
THE COSMOPOLITAN

This yummy pink libation was created in 1987 at the trendy New York hangout, the Odeon. It was the drink of choice for the gals on Sex and the City *and represented the revival of the cocktail, making mixed drinks from martinis to mojitos chic again. Here's how to shake one up:*

1-1/4 oz. vodka
1/4 oz. triple sec
1/4 oz. lime juice
1/4 oz. cranberry juice

Combine all ingredients with one cup ice cubes in cocktail shaker; shake well. Strain into martini glass.

DINNER, ANYONE?

Now that you've mastered cocktails, it's time to tackle a sit-down dinner. According to etiquette expert Peggy Post, most people consider a formal dinner to be one where guests are seated at a dining table and "the entire meal is served by someone other than themselves." (Hmm . . . moms across the country do this on a nightly basis!) Actually, as Peggy Post points out, the big difference between formal and informal is how many courses are served and how the table is set. Some guidelines follow.

The Formal Dinner

A formal dinner traditionally includes as many as six courses:

Soup, fruit cup or melon, or shellfish

Fish (unless shellfish is served first)
or sweetbreads

Entrée, with vegetables

Salad

Dessert

Coffee and after-dinner drinks

The number of courses dictates the table setting, as each course will have its own silver. A formal place setting usually includes the following:

SERVICE PLATE OR CHARGER: Set out first, this serves as an underplate for the first and second courses, which are brought out on separate dishes. The service plate remains when the first and second course dishes are removed, and is taken away when the entrée is served.

BUTTER PLATE: Placed above the forks on the left side.

SALAD FORK: Unless the salad is served first, the salad fork goes on the left, closest to the service plate.

DINNER FORK: Placed to the left of the salad fork, and used for the entrée course.

FISH FORK: If there is a fish course, this fork is placed farthest to the left.

DINNER KNIFE: Placed to the right of the service plate.

FISH KNIFE: If fish is served, this specially shaped knife goes next, to the right of the dinner knife.

BUTTER KNIFE: Placed diagonally on top of the butter plate.

SOUP SPOON OR FRUIT SPOON: If the first course is soup or fruit, the proper spoon would go to the right of the knives.

OYSTER FORK: If serving shellfish, this fork would go to the right of the spoons. No other fork is ever placed on the right.

CRYSTAL: A formal table setting includes several glasses, placed directly above the knives on the right hand side, and arranged by size: a water goblet; the red wine glass next; and then the white wine glass. Other glasses may also be added, such as a champagne flute or sherry glass.

The Informal Sit-Down Meal

This usually consists of two to three courses including an appetizer, such as soup or salad; main course and side dishes; and dessert. The table is easy to make sense of, and calls for only a few utensils, which are placed in the order they are used—from the outside in. With few exceptions, forks go on the left of the plate, knives and spoons to the right.

Whether you are hosting a formal or casual dinner, plates and corresponding silver should be cleared from the table after each course and never passed, stacked, or—heaven forbid—scraped at the table! Bread plates and knives are left on the table until the dessert course. If someone has used the wrong utensil, don't ask them to hold onto it. Remove it, and then replace it with a fresh one.

Bubbly Bath

There's nothing that signals festive elegance like champagne, and nothing that can ruin the experience faster than sipping it warm. In a pinch, you can quick-cool champagne in about twenty minutes by submerging the bottle in a bucket filled with ice and water. The ice water will help chill it faster than ice alone.

ELEGANT TOUCHES FOR YOUR TABLE

Whether dining with friends or entertaining business associates, consider the following elegant options:

MATCHING CHAIRS ARE A MUST

Most sit-down affairs will include between six and ten guests. If you don't have enough chairs that match, consider renting them.

TABLE LINENS

A white damask tablecloth and matching napkins are the traditional choice for a formal dinner party. Linen cloths are also fine, but no matter what you choose, make sure your linens are clean and pressed. Renting linens is a reasonable option, as the price is often not much more than what it would cost to have your own laundered. A word about napkins: they

should be folded and placed on the center of the plates, or on the left of (and not under) the forks.

CANDLES

White tapers are classically elegant, and should be lit before the guests arrive, remaining lit until after they leave.

DON'T FORGET THE CENTERPIECE

Fresh flowers are always an option, but keep them low. Huge arrangements are overkill, and impossible to see through.

PLACE CARDS HAVE THEIR PLACE

Place cards add an elegant and formal flair to the meal, but they don't have to be stuffy. Try something fun like using a digital, black and white photo of the person instead of their name. Or choose a small frame to hold the place card, which can also serve as a party gift.

shabby chic

Style can't be purchased.

ANDY SPADE,
HUSBAND OF STYLE GURU, KATE SPADE

ELEGANCE ON A BUDGET

Real life and money matters have a way of reining in our grand plans and lofty visions. But that doesn't mean you have to give up on elegance. Picking and choosing how to spend your time and money can actually help define your own style. Having limited resources will force you to focus a discerning eye when choosing one thing (whether an item of clothing, piece of furniture, or package of stationery) over another. The trick is to choose wisely, and don't be afraid to look for creative solutions to your budgeting challenges. Necessity is the mother of invention. (See Accidental Elegance on page 129.) But remember— sometimes it makes practical sense to spend

a little more in the short run for something that will pay off in the long run. So when is it okay to splurge?

Spend on classics—items you think will hold up and be in style for several years: a cashmere turtleneck, a fine leather purse, a high quality sofa. Cut corners on things you know you'll probably end up replacing: gloves, sunglasses, a rug you know your kids are going to destroy. Don't buy something on sale without considering whether you'd actually still buy it (and enjoy it) if it weren't such a bargain.

Things That Aren't Bargains,
AT ANY PRICE

- Half-price Manolo Blahniks, which happen to hurt your feet.

- Cashmere jacket, reduced because the lining is completely ripped. Are you really going to get it repaired?

- Anything that has a funny odor when you buy it.

- Shopworn "sample" items or floor models. The shoe on display, for example, may be faded compared to its mate.

- Bulk items of staples like paper towels, toilet paper etc., that are "dirt cheap," but you have no room to store. Say NO, or you'll be saying yes to clutter.

- An item your best friend or salesperson has talked you into. Not only is this not a bargain, it's a full blown mistake. If you need someone else's opinion, you're probably not "in love."

ACCESSIBLE CHIC

Ways to stretch your
dollar without looking
like you did:

Shop Online

Online clothing, furniture, and accessory
sites are often less expensive than retail out-
lets. Satisfaction is practically guaranteed if
you've seen or tried on an item in a store
first, and then purchase it online. Some sites
even offer free shipping for orders over a
small minimum.

Shop at Auction

Auctions, especially online versions, offer
bargains on all sorts of items, such as name
brand purses and luggage.

Consider Cashing in Miles

Did you know you can exchange the points

or miles you've earned on your credit card for gift certificates to many retail stores? Check with your credit card company for details.

Get Out Your Sewing Machine, or Visit the Tailor

A nip here or a tuck there can do wonders for last year's suit jacket, or turn that formal gown into a cocktail dress you'll really wear. Note: Not everything is worth fixing. Don't spend a lot to re-purpose inexpensive or worn items, or things that are hopelessly out of date.

Skip the Fillet, Splurge on the Soufflé

When throwing a dinner party, don't spend a fortune or tons of time on every course. Choose easy recipes and reasonably priced ingredients for your appetizers and entrée. Then splurge on a great bottle of wine, and spend your effort on dessert. It will leave guests with a delicious last impression.

Put a Frame on It

Framing and hanging special objects and personal artwork is one of the easiest ways to express your personal style. You'll be surprised how beautiful almost any treasure will look (your child's artwork, a vintage silk scarf, a meaningful letter or retro postcard) when you frame it.

Accidental Elegance

As a mother of two young children, Rachel Ashwell needed a practical yet charming way to protect her furniture and decorate her home. The slipcovers she used, made of natural fabrics, were so sought after by admiring friends, they became the basis for her own line of furnishings. Ashwell's company, "Shabby Chic," has since become synonymous with modern, easy elegance.

Simply Chic

Speaking of easy elegance, here are a month's worth of ideas to nurture elegance, one day at a time:

Day 1: Learn one French (or Spanish, or German) word today.

Day 2: Drink your coffee or tea from a cup with a saucer.

Day 3: Rent *Breakfast at Tiffany's*.

Day 4: Write a note instead of sending an e-mail.

Day 5: Use a silver mint julep cup to hold cotton swabs or pencils.

Day 6: Thank someone you wouldn't normally thank for something they've done.

Day 7: Curl up with Edith Wharton's novel, *The Age of Innocence*.

Day 8: Donate books or magazines to a library or nursing home.

Day 9: Write down something you are grateful for.

Day 10: Use your "fancy" soap and hand towels, instead of saving them for company.

Day 11: Read a poem.

Day 12: Write a poem. (You don't have to show it to anyone.)

Day 13: In front of a mirror, practice standing up straight.

Day 14: Do something childish: color, play jacks, eat a popsicle.

Day 15: Pick some flowers, and put them by your bed.

Day 16: Eat in the dining room
         tonight.

Day 17: Write a letter to someone
         who mentored you.

Day 18: Refrain from gossiping.

Day 19: Shop or run an errand
         for an elderly neighbor.

Day 20: Buy yourself a gift, for
         no reason.

Day 21: Buy someone else a gift,
         for no reason.

Day 22: Read a biography of someone
         you find particularly elegant.

Day 23: Take your daughter or a
         friend out for tea.

Day 24: Line your lingerie drawer.

Day 25:   Instead of browsing through
           the latest catalog, grab an art
           book instead.

Day 26:   Notice something beautiful in
           nature: an exquisite color, or
           the flight of a bird.

Day 27:   Frame a quote that moves
           you. Hang it in your office,
           or near the phone.

Day 28:   Pull your pearls out of storage
           and wear them.

Day 29:   Make a conscious choice
           to listen to a new CD or
           radio station.

Day 30:   Do something
           just for fun: joy
           is a priceless
           accessory!

the write stuff

I am convinced more and more day by day that fine writing is next to fine doing, the top thing in the world.

JOHN KEATS

GRACE NOTES

There's no better way to practice the art of elegance than to send a handwritten note. It's one of the surest ways to make you, and the person you're writing to, feel special and connected. Writing a note is the proper and most elegant way to thank someone for a thoughtful gift or kind act, or to share in a time of joy or sorrow. The fact that fewer and fewer people seem to take the time to write notes only makes them more special. If you're not convinced, consider the following benefits of the handwritten note:

● When you write a note, you've taken care of an obligation or desire. You can truly "cross it off your list." Trading messages on phone answering machines doesn't always accomplish this. And e-mails are a dime a dozen. Yours may go unread, at least for a few days.

Handwritten notes are, by their nature, personal. They can also be beautiful. Consequently, they almost always pack a more impressive, lasting punch than other forms of communication. You can still use technology to help you keep up with everyday chores like scheduling activities or staying in touch. But when you want your words to matter, write them by hand.

TIMING IS EVERYTHING

One of the most challenging aspects of writing notes is finding the time to compose a thoughtful one. If you're like most people, time, or lack thereof, will be the one thing that keeps you from putting pen to paper. The best way to handle this, of course, is to tackle the note right away. (This way, you'll avoid starting off with, "Sorry this is so late . . . ") In addition, your sentiments will be fresh in your mind, and will make the note easier to compose. Most important, you won't miss the window of opportunity to get the note out the door and in the mail. But if you do put it off, how late is too late?

THANK YOU NOTES

According to etiquette expert Peggy Post, thank you notes should arrive no later than a week after the gift is received. The exceptions are wedding or shower gifts, where dozens of notes must be written. The accepted time limit for a wedding thank you, for example, is three months from the receipt of the gift.

Maybe you're wondering whether you should send a note at all, and that's what's holding you up. According to Post, it's never wrong to send a thank you note. But sometimes it isn't necessary. For instance, there is no need to send a note if you've already thanked the giver in person (except again, for formal affairs like those mentioned above). You also don't have to send a note to thank a host or hostess for dinner, although if you were an overnight guest, a note is a must. The bottom line: when in doubt, send one out.

LETTERS OF SYMPATHY

In most cases, a condolence note should be sent within a week or so after learning of the death. But it is not wrong to send one weeks, or even months later. Just tell the person you've been thinking of them, and wanted to let them know.

WRITTEN REPLIES TO PARTIES OR WEDDINGS

Observe "RSVP by" dates. If no date is given, respond within three days, especially if you are unable to attend. This way the hosts will have time to invite someone else if they desire.

WRITE ON

If you want to increase your chances of actually writing a note, and getting it out on time, look no farther than your stationery drawer. Having the right stationery, easily accessible, is the best way to ensure that you'll actually sit down and get the job done. In addition, make sure that your address book, stamps, and a pen are nearby.

Stationery Wardrobe
THE WELL-DRESSED DESK

Picking out stationery is a little like shopping for a bra: there are so many styles to choose from, but it's hard to find one that fits. Don't despair. The following stationery choices will offer you just the right amount of support for all your letter-writing needs.

MONARCH SHEETS

Slightly smaller than traditional business letterhead, a monarch sheet measures 7-1/4 by 10-1/2 inches. Although technically not the most formal stationery you can own, it can cover all your formal needs. Sheets are folded into thirds to fit the accompanying envelope.

CORRESPONDENCE CARDS

This "little black dress" of your desk drawer can be used for both business and personal matters. Write only on the front of the card; it's considered improper to use the back. May be imprinted or engraved with your name, initials, or decorative icon.

FOLDOVER NOTES

Decorative note cards are versatile and also make great gifts. The inside "blank" is used to write thank you's, gift enclosures, or other casual correspondence.

Despite their name, they are the most formal of the group. Informals differ from other foldover notes in that they come only in white or ecru paper. They are engraved or embossed with your name on the front.

You need not invest in all of these variations. In fact, stocking your drawer with just one set of personalized correspondence cards and envelopes will be enough to get you started. Once you've gotten your stationery in place, writing the note will be a cinch.

beauty from the inside out

*A truly elegant taste is generally
accompanied by excellence of heart.*

HENRY FIELDING

STAND UP STRAIGHT

Charm school and posture lessons may be out of vogue. But when it comes to striking a chic pose, you'll fall flat on your face if you don't consider your carriage, and the message it sends. Standing up straight is one of the easiest things you can do to transform yourself and your outfit from frumpy to fabulous. Standing tall says "confidence" and exudes optimism. On the other hand, if everything about you droops, you look tired and discouraged, not to mention older and heavier than you really are.

Start with your stomach. Pull it back to your spine—not your lungs. Shoulders should be back, but relaxed, not stiff or strained. Your chest should be neither hidden nor pushed forward (this will throw your back off).

Hold your head high. Picture a graceful ballerina, or even how you hold yourself when trying on new clothes; you innately know that when you stand up straight your clothes look better on you.

When striking an elegant stance, pay attention if something hurts or feels strained. You may be standing unnaturally straight or taut, or need to work on muscle strength and flexibility. Your everyday activities, such as how you sit, sleep, stand, or even talk on the phone, can affect your posture and health. Poor alignment can put pressure on your back and joints, causing pain and fatigue. So stand tall. Not only does it make you look good, it's good for you.

Body Language

Posture is one of the first three things people notice about us. (The other two are hair and eyes.)

MIND YOUR MANNERS

The topic of etiquette has enjoyed a renewed interest of late. You can find advice on everything from table manners for teens to teaching toddlers  the basics of thank you notes. And there's a good reason for all the fuss: good manners make the difference. Manners and proper etiquette aren't mandatory subjects anymore, but they should be. When distracted by our hectic lives, the rules of etiquette remind us to make time to be courteous and thoughtful of others. In addition, exercising good manners can help us notice and appreciate life's special moments instead of just speeding by them.

People are sometimes put off by the idea of manners, and associate etiquette with rules for high society. (In fact, the word etiquette may have come from a French word for signs—*etiquettes*—some of which requested the courtiers at the Versailles palace of Louis XIV to keep off the grass!) But the truth is, modern manners are meant to steer us through everyday rituals and routines, as well as formal occasions. Consider these everyday tenets:

- Be considerate of others—their space, their time, their feelings.

- Make others feel at ease; it's Etiquette 101.

- Say what you mean, and do what you say. In other words, be honest and true.

- Listen to Aretha Franklin, and show some r-e-s-p-e-c-t for those around you and yourself.

- Practice your pleases and thank you's. Even grown-ups need to be reminded from time to time.

- Strive for graciousness, and don't forget to be flexible.

- Table your bad habits: keep your elbows off, don't talk with your mouth full, put your napkin in your lap!

- Kindness is contagious. Make sure to spread some around.

- Good manners will take you everywhere, so don't go anywhere without them.

LAUGH LINES

Acting properly doesn't rule out cutting up and having fun. In fact, laughing (especially at your own foibles) is one of the classiest acts in the book. Having a sense of humor about yourself and life in general will do more to lighten your load and enrich your daily experience than any other trick you might try. That's a pretty grand claim, but as anyone knows who has ever rolled on the floor, holding their sides in glee, laughter is truly the best medicine.

Laughter works in a number of ways. First, it's a powerful communication tool. It helps us engage with others, and puts those we're interacting with at ease. It's literally the voice of joy. Who wouldn't want more of that in their lives? Humor also adds levity to difficult or uncomfortable situations, helping us put problems into perspective so we can deal with them more effectively.

A good laugh not only helps us, psychologically speaking, it's also good for us physiologically. Studies have shown that laughing, like other forms of exercise, increases heart and respiration rates, oxygenates our bodies, and reduces stress hormones. The result is a more resilient immune system, which may actually help us fight disease. In addition, many argue that laughing can produce a "eustress state," a feeling of well-being that is like a runner's high. So the next time something goes wrong, whether you break a heel or lose an important account, see if you can't find a way to laugh about it. Humor will turn a loss into a win every time.

elegant endings

Every exit is an entry somewhere else.

TOM STOPPARD,
ROSENCRANTZ AND GUILDENSTERN ARE DEAD

HOW TO SAY GOODBYE

All good things must come to an end, so why is saying goodbye so hard? Transitions are difficult because the unknown is scary. Many people get anxious over new beginnings, but more of us shudder at endings. (Fearing the devil you know is better than the devil you don't.) But end things we must, whether it's a relationship that's run its course, or even a chapter in our lives, like being single. Bidding adieu gracefully is the best way to start fresh and embrace what lies ahead.

Breaking Up is Hard to Do

Ending a relationship, either a friendship or romantic liaison, is often painful and hard to face. It's no wonder that many of us put off the unpleasantness, which of course just makes things worse. When breaking off a romance, take some pressure off the situation by realizing that if your heart isn't in it, your soon-to-be ex will be better off with someone else. That doesn't mean you should start the conversation with: "Listen, I'm really doing you a favor . . . " If you're the one breaking it off, it's your responsibility to do so in a way that shows genuine concern for the other person. No matter how hard or uncomfortable the situation, observe these basic courtesies:

1. MEET IN PERSON, AND IN PRIVATE

If someone deserved enough of your time to merit a relationship, they also deserve a face-to-face meeting. It's the height of rudeness and cowardice to break up via letter, e-mail, or worse yet, as was the case with one of

 Carrie Bradshaw's suitors, by leaving a message on a Post-it note! The phone should only be used as a last resort, when timing or distance makes a one-on-one

impossible. (But never leave the bad news on someone's answering machine.) And when you do meet, be decent enough to avoid a place crowded with other people.

2. KEEP IT SHORT AND SWEET

Remember, you're trying to spare someone else's feelings, not justify your own. Get to the point, and be kind. There is no need to point out all the horrible things you detest about the other person—it's cruel and vindictive. And don't make up excuses either. For a short-lived relationship, you can explain that you're sorry, "but things just aren't working out," or you're "not ready for the relation-ship." With longer term affairs, honesty, tem-pered with tact, is the best policy.

3. SHOW RESPECT WITHOUT LETTING THINGS LINGER

Once you've made the break, don't keep checking in to see if everything's okay, or try to switch to friendship mode too quickly.

Give the other person time to process and move on. Remember that how you talk about the relationship to others after it's over will reflect more on YOU than on your ex. So be discreet, classy, and respectful.

Dear John, Who Are You?

No one wants to be the recipient of a "Dear John" letter. But exactly who was "John," anyway? The term came about during World War II, referring to the letters written to soldiers overseas by wives and girlfriends who found their love couldn't survive the distance.

Breaking Up with a Friend

Ending a friendship can be much more difficult and painful than a romantic break-up. The whole idea of dating implies that you're looking for someone who is the right fit. If it doesn't work out, it's assumed you just haven't found the one. But friendships are entered into differently, and the rules for ending one are murky. Although the basic considerations apply, such as being kind and thoughtful of the other person's feelings, sometimes it's better to let friendships run their course, fading naturally, rather than abruptly calling it quits. If you're always unavailable or busy, the other person will get the drift. They will also be free to interpret your absence as they wish, without necessarily taking it personally.

Saying Goodbye to a Colleague or Friend Who's Moving

Parting *can* be such sweet sorrow (if both parties are still fond of each other). And as with

so many other things, it's often hard to find the time to acknowledge the occasion. Marking the departure in some way helps to close one chapter and start a new one. Consider these ways to mark the moment:

HOST A GOING-AWAY CELEBRATION

It can be something as small as taking the other person out for coffee, or a full blown going-away party.

SAY IT WITH PICTURES

Frame a special photo, make an album, or even a T-shirt that will remind the person of the good times you've spent together. Or take a picture on the day they leave, and send it to them later.

PLAN A CONCRETE TIME TO SEE EACH OTHER AGAIN

Make it happen with a commitment, such as getting tickets to an upcoming event, or inviting them to a birthday celebration.

PUT IT IN WRITING

Even a simple card will help commemorate
the moment. Consider attaching a small
gift, such as something for their new surroundings.

GIVE NOTICE

When you're the one who's leaving, give
friends, colleagues and neighbors plenty of
notice. It will give them time to plan for
their goodbyes to you.

I Quit!

Leaving a job nowadays is not nearly as rare
or taboo as it once was. People move around
all the time, but that doesn't mean leaving a
post is easy. Quitting with class is a skill
worth acquiring. After all, you never know
when you might run into each other again.

When it's obvious to both you and your
boss that things aren't working out, be proac-

tive. If you wait around to be let go, you risk being caught without a back-up plan.

Two weeks notice is the minimum required if you want to leave on good terms, but more time is often appreciated. Be prepared to make your contacts and files available to whoever is taking your place.

Thanking your boss for the positive things you got from the experience, rather than rattling off a list of grievances, will help leave the door open for the future, should you ever want to return or work for that person again.

Don't bad-mouth your boss or company when you leave. Again, you will come off in a much better light if you focus on the future rather than dishing about the past.

THE PARTY'S OVER

The dessert's been served, and the coffee passed. Are we done yet? When is it time to go home? If you're a guest at someone else's house, the rules are simple. It is common din-  ner party courtesy for guests to stay awhile after dinner is served, usually an hour or so. But after that, pay attention to the vibe, and any subtle hints from the host. Unless the host specifically requests you to stay, leave when everyone else does. Cocktail parties are less rigid, and people often come and go more freely. The main thing to remember is whatever the occasion, don't overstay your welcome. Make sure to personally thank your hosts before you leave. Thanking them twice is even better.

Now for the trickier issue. How do you give a guest who stays too long the boot?

Although it's generally best to leave the dishes until after guests go, starting to clean up may help give hangers-on the message. If this or other gentle hints don't work (like yawns or talk of your early morning plans) you may have to be a little more obvious. It's okay to give people a nudge by saying something like "I'm not as young as I use to be, I've got to get to bed!" If your guests still won't leave, your only choice is to throw them a pillow, shut off the lights, and take their refusal to budge as the ultimate compliment. It may not be the perfect ending, but it was probably a heck of a party. Job well done.